Mosaics

Premiere Partie

Brittany Bronte

A Dedication

For Shanleigh and Tristan-

*Always find the beauty
Even the beauties hidden, within the many moments
of your lives.*

Mosaics

Partie Un

A mosaic is often formed by bits of sharded glass in an array of patterns and colors. Such is our lives- the moments that make us who we are.
Mosaics is a collection of poems about memories, motherhood, and experiences of learning and growing.
Human beings share emotions and experiences, and coming together, can find solace and connection through each other.

It is my hope the reader finds solace and connection here.

The Radio

Rubbing the wood

Until it shines

Like the sun beams

That dance

Down from the window

How did we get so lucky?

To have peace

And music

On a beautiful morning

In this shoebox

We call home

Judy

How do you know?

That I am not good enough

That I am damaged

You are so wise to see

I deserve that you

Throw balls at me

To make me move

That you call me ugly

You see the truth, after all

I do not deserve food or kindness

I am here

Because I am not wanted, after all

And on the wood floor

Under the dining room table

Asleep and in my dreams

You kicked my teeth in

And quiet as a mouse

I swallowed them down

And drifted back to sleep

Lonely Hearts Club

Made just for me
By your hands
My first music
And I devoured it
Thinking somewhere between the cords
It held the secrets to your heart

First Love

With Flowers in her hair and the wind in her eyes
She steals my love away
She rode to the sun in her chariot of fire
And my desire
Was burnt to the snow
She blew away the ashes with the breath from her lips
And with her open hips
Carried him to her sun

Inspiration

A million little loves descend from heaven

With their golden wings

And flaxen hair

All wrapped in the morning

They dance around my fingers

With their prickly touch

They fill my eyes

ooze into my ears

And dance

And sing

I'll keep them here forever

All my million loves

Childhood

Let the sun fill our eyes

And the dew kiss our feet

As we dance in the meadow

And rejoice for the dead

Take my hand

Lift me up

To caress the stars with my tongue

The wind and its secrets

Pour into my ears

For one last time

I will vanish in this world

Wanderlust

In the North Country is where my home lies
And in the California sun
My home is nestled in a schoolboy's heart
And arise in the colors of a masterpiece of art
My best friend is the howling wind
And the glisten in a spring rain shower
And the old town clock that chimes every hour
Is my prayer to her
My dreams fade at the end of every smoke
And hide in the thoughts of a fresh born babe
My hopes are the fault of a poet's tongue
And rest on the best of an American drum
Silhouetting against our sunrise- I rise and fall
Think of me beyond the horizon of the sun
And we will be as one

Schizophrenia

Sour mind
Frozen in time
Glued hands
Where I stand
Scared look
"I'll read a book"
Words fly
As I watch myself die
Cannot express
Through all this mess
I'll pass this test
If God loves me

I'll give it a whirl
For the taste of a pearl
And the arms of the world
To fold around me
When I look in his eyes
I feel my spirits rise
And crumble on his lips
All I want is his kiss
I'd give my soul
With all its holes
And every drop of my blood
If I only could
For a little silence

Virginity

He had an eye full of smiles
The warmth of the sun
And I should have broken all ties
With that fight
But I thought I had won

Every second was spent with him
The rotations of the moon
Love was nestling in my brain
Though I knew it was too soon

We would visit all the places
All over this green Earth
I would awake in Mexico
He'd be challenging the surf

A gift I gave- I thought he would cherish
He told me of our life
And a time for marriage

But I knew it wouldn't be
For the smiles had stopped
Now it's all lies
And not what I hoped

That gift I never gave
To anyone else
I gave it to him
Every piece of myself

The Marine

Strolling by the ocean-blue
I wonder if my love- so true
Is smiling inside because one day- sweet
He knows in his head that his heart is complete
Will this be what it will take?
For him to make
The decision to come home
After a long road traveled alone?

Daughter

Where did you go

During the times that were hard

We were so close

When that man

Pushed you out of my heart

I relied on your strength

Maybe too much?

Where did the child go?

Now a woman before me

Heredity

The invisible luggage

Of collected misdeeds

You've been gathering all these years

Do not recycle them

And make them yours

Letter to My Son

Why can't you be only mine?

My heart, the heart I trust

To grow you and love you

To let you be you

And not an extension

of my hopes, dreams, and successes

I let you be you

No strings attached

Music

A familiar song
A memory of yourself
And you whisper down
"You're going to be ok"

A familiar song
Can reach down
And pull you out
To meet yourself again

Old Friend

Sometimes music feels like an old friend
Whose been waiting to see you
And all your stress melts away
Shedding like a winter coat
In the summer sun

The Son

The question of unguarded moments
Who will bubble up to the lines of his face?
Will I see myself or the father?

Unspoken

Cannot swallow
anything but disappointments
When did my adorations
turn into loathing?
When did the victim
begin to look like
the aggressor?

Life

Like a tattered quilt
Each square an experience
Separated and disjointed
But together wrap me in comfort
Each having a part to play
In keeping the quilt together

The Doctor

Spinning
Your face
Like a rock
Amidst the waves
You anchor me down
And help me
Set my feet
Upon the ground

Words

When they fall like a stone
Sudden and with a thud
Catching your feet
Refusing to be overlooked

When they drift upwards
Like a feather
In the wind
Not caring where they fall
Like they were never said at all

The Cracker Jack

All the hopes in the world
Rest on 2 quarters
so easy to spend so cheaply
When you don't know the value of yourself

Trying to make it work
Adding a bit of glue
And applying a bit of tape
To hide the bumps and the scrapes

You hold it up
Comparing it to your friends
It plays - sort of
It bends- kind of
Living a life of parallels

Something is different
What could it be?
The color is the same
The size is the same

And then you realize
It is simply…
Love

Obligation and Love

You can have one
Without the other
You can't have the other
without the one

Borrowed Time

When you cannot see a future
And you only see today
When tomorrow is not promised
Priorities are simple
Live
Laugh
And Play
But life is hard
For the one
That is carrying you

Choice

One door is for a key
Of predictability
Stability
For the house that stands
Made of bricks
But feels like sand

One door is for a key
Of myself
An uncharted sea
Of unpredictability
A house built of strength
And knowing it's maker

Open Road

On the open road
The story goes
Light and free
Like a summer breeze
Where will it blow me
To a place of my dreams?
Even a tree is something special
In an unfamiliar place

Time

Time moves
But people choose
To live
And relive
To be born
And reborn

Am I a spec within
The continuity of it all?

Or do I resonate
As does
The whispers of my heart?

Age

The warm sun on my face
A soft and safe place
Not caring to win the race
I set the pace
For beauty and grace
Like on a bride, the lace
That drifts in waves and folds
A softness to behold
And I remember what was told
You are only as old
As your soul knows

The Awakening

Quiet, my fiery soul
Appease the dragon
And lay dormant
The life I created will crumble.
And what will emerge from the ruins?

Parasite

Like slime in a jar
Oozing
Creeping and silent
You fill the space
Sucking up all the air
Around my face

Borrowed Glasses

Seeking someone
To see yourself through
Borrowing their perspective
Because you are unable
To see yourself

The Builder

Building a house
With the lies I told myself
That you whispered in my ear
I tell myself
"It just 1 or 2 bad bricks"
"There's enough mortar to keep it strong"
Until I realize the house
With all it's rooms
And birthday parties
And home-made cookie smell
It's been built on dreams
And like a loan
I was waiting for the check
To pay it off
And make it real

The Gift

An unfinished bath tray

Sitting there

Waiting for me to earn it

"Maybe I should do it myself?"

But no- I let it sit

And be a glowing reminder

Of the manipulation

That I am walking away from

The Candle

A woman

Full and independent

Yearning and powerful

A Man

Thoughtful and persistent

A provider and A father

"When the candle is lit-

I can give to you..."

In control, I thought

Being in control means giving freely

Because I am strong enough to do without

But you were supposed to keep me

From giving away pieces of myself

You were supposed to keep me

From becoming nothing

My candle is out

You are not welcome

There is nothing left to give

Beware, the Vultures

Did you know

There are vultures

who are disguised as people

Walking around

On the hunt

Looking into your soul

To offer you your desires

And only for the moment

To tear your words into shreds

And to wear your skin

Leaving you stripped

Of what was once yourself

Beware, the vultures

Words

Like a painting for our ears

Portraits of pain

And what it is to be human

Brilliant and somber

colors that sing

And tickle the eardrum

Reaching deep inside

to squeeze the heart

Peaches

Ripe and for the taking

Firm and soft in your hands

Take a bite

My skin will bite back

The Clock

Around the room

Fists clenched

and only half

wanting a resolution

The other half

Wanting a fight

Where were you

When the words flew

And hit me

Across my face

As the clock ticks

And marks the time

Into another day

The Photograph

You don't see me

Carrying all the weight

For a happy home

You don't see me

Carrying all the blame

For what goes wrong

You only see

A photograph you are given

By someone who loves you

And who's supposed

To love me too

The Tree

You and me

Up in the tree

Where we shared our secrets

You took your two fingers

And touched the part

That was supposed to be just for myself

And I felt the sky crumble

And turn black

As you waited for my answer

Thank you

You said thank you

Like it wasn't going

To cost you a thing

Like the kindness

You accepted

Didn't come with strings

The Loss

In those childhood moments

When you know your parents were near

And you drift to sleep

That silent and knowing security

You were always there

Living a parallel life

Keeping the world on its axis

Of positivity

Now you are gone

We didn't know you

But we felt you there

And now we feel

The loss

of a world without you

A Woman's Choice

Holding my breath

And clenching my teeth

Determined to give it away

You were as gentle

As you could be

A boy without a name

And me with my child-like Frame

When the pain was too much

You help me in your arms

And I felt like a failure

Social Anxiety

Chained down

My tongue

A prisoner of my own

Whose words

Are these

Flying out of my mouth

Can you feel it

The pleading

Behind my eyes

The perspective you have

Is not the one

I am trying to paint

How many moments

Will be blown

Until they are all spent?

How many more

Do I have left

To get it right

A Therapist's Work

You say plainly

Words of observation

As easily as if you are calling

A crow, black.

But to me

Your words become discoveries

Like unearthing a rare ruby

Or climbing Mt. Everest

You chisel away

At the hard pieces

And I steady my feet

For the last leg of the climb

All the while

On your worn, leather couch

And you right there

Never leaving your chair

Perspective

When the tragedies

could be opportunities

And the defeats

Could be retreats

Into the

D

E

E

P

Parts of yourself

To find the strength

You have tucked away

And like a cowboy

Wrangle it up

And bring it out

To face the day

For the Empath

Spilling out

All over the place

Raw and oozing

Splattering on the floor

My heart swelling with every word I hear

And overflowing with every word I say

How do I bind it up

And patch up the holes

Keeping contained

All that I am

Negativity

Your attitude is a sickness

Like a contagion

And to be me again

I scrub myself clean

And let you go

The Expectation

Sit with it

The disappointment

Of a dangling conversation

And set a course

For steering you back

Where smiles are shared

And the conversations pile up

Like pieces of art

The Last Night

Under the moon
At the speed of light
That stillness of the night
Wraps us up

In that little red truck
with wings for wheels
I ask you about the stars
And you give an answer
Like you don't even hear

I take your answer
And cherish it anyway
A child's heart
doesn't have expectations

Two Sisters

The day we were locked out

Of the trailer on the hill

On that summer's afternoon

I had trees and hills and fields and flowers

And My imagination

So I had everything

But I did not understand

Why you were afraid

Summer

Banners in the wind

Billowing in white

Smells of clean

And grass

And sunshine

My bare feet covered

in evidence of play

These are the days

Of freedom

And innocence

The Piano

Across the room

With your white smile

Offering yourself

For a chance to sing

Oh how I could

Settle myself down

And tickle your keys

To make you scream

If only to create a sound

That stretches and fills

The empty spaces

Of this place

The Rally

Watching the days pile up

Of my own life

Like being the side act

In my own play

I'd like to scoop them up

And rewrite them

Like a collection of alternate endings

I'd write myself in

With the confidence

To steal the scene

Every time

The Mild Afternoon

The scent of a shy sunshine

Smells of hope

And a promise

For a better tomorrow

Elating my heart

And along it beats

With the rise and fall

Of the gentle breeze

Conversation with a Narcissist

Like a monologue

Of the ultimate

Performer

And your applause

Is an expected part of the show

Like a game

Being played

With only one team

And the pitches you toss

Fall with a thud to the ground

And like a book

With only one

Side of the story

And all the other characters

Have been written out

A New Day

New eyes

Seeing you

Detached

From the emotion

That use to drown me

And make me feel

Like the waves were from the chaos

I created

New eyes

Seeing you

With destruction

Signed

By your name

While the dust settles to look for blame

New eyes

Seeing you

With your sadness

And leaving you

With the bags

You made me carry

That I filled with tears

The Afternoon

Open hips

In his hands

Sweet nectar

Overflows

Dining

On my lips

Dying

And being

Reborn

All at once

Gnawing moments

Gnawing Moments

Of subtle importance

The simplicity of

A child's laughter

And barefeet

Pitter-Patter

A breeze whispers

Remember this day

The time stands still for you

Stopping to smell the roses

And I notice

The ordinary beauty

Of a regular afternoon

In the life of a child

On the day I was a mother

The Dream

Making ready

To bury your head

Quick work

Out of respect and need

Preparing a place

Where you can't watch me

And torment me

Or nip at my heels

The rot is beginning

No time to waste

To put you away

Forever rested

Out of my light

And outside

Of my line of sight

The Message

Did you get my message?

And you mean

Why didn't you message back?

The way you look at me

Like all the hurdles for miles

Can be knocked down and moved out of our way

By your message

And the response

You imagine you deserve

The Blueprint

Quiet Strength

Gentle smile

Pools of depth

In your eyes

Open hands

Soft and slow

Patient

And knowing

Driven by the need

To be a good man

And understanding the model

Of being a good father

And for a son and daughter

Giving a gift...

To love their mother

Petrified

Straight and clean

Branches

Reaching up from roots

Every season

The circumstances

Overcome by truth

A mirror of strength

A memory of our youth

Grow and grow some more

Despite me

You and I are strong

From needing to be free

And the resilience of a living thing

That can no longer bleed

Pay Day

Tending to my art

Like I tend to my money

When the deposit hits

Feverishly creating

Like the mood with evaporate

As if it always leaves me waiting

The Wedding

Part 1

Facing you

Clasping hands

The hopes of future years

Hanging in our eyes

Overwhelming

And electrifying

Filling up

Like a balloon

Swelling up

The love between us

Part 2

The years ahead

Hold their secrets

They share in whispers

With the flowers

But my feet

Are too light

And my feet

Are too fast

To hear them

Part 3

If I had my life

To live over

I would not live

For dreams

On your shoulders

They were heavy

And you crumbled

Under the weight of them

And at my feet

Laid the blame

The Sun

Slowly rising

Like my strength

When the luxury of choice

Is not an option

Sisters facing

With the consternation

Of a knowing

Determination

Live or die this way

I say- all the while dawning

That dying is not an option

Like the burning out

Of the sun

My Brothers

Like the warmth of the sun in the morning

Little whispers spread

Beckoning me to the canopies

Of living trees and leaf beds

Wrapping around my shoulders

A welcoming embrace

Sending all the stress and worry

Away without a trace

My brothers standing strong and towery

With me in our shade

Goodbye

Packing away

The dreams of the day

Putting back

The hopes that I have

Storing up

Energy that is retrofit

And I need every bit

Not wasting one drip

On you anymore

Farewell and it was nice

Trying on the visions

I had for our lives

Wearing the figments

Of my imagination

Waves of fabric and fabrications

Wafting around

And leaving the impression

That you like the way

They look on me

Cypress

Tall, proud, and regal

Towering over

With bended spender and grace

Thick folds of moss

Draping over your gnarly face

Time stands still for you

Soaking up the years like a day

Offering wisdom

In whispers on the breeze

Being shared throughout the leaves

Anecdotes of lessons learned from histories

And if we stand very still and listen

We might learn what it takes

To save Mother Earth

Before she brakes

Take the Horns of the Bull

Take the horns of the bull

And charge

Until the walls you built around yourself

Fall

For on the other side

A path awaits

Lit by the light of the moon

Take the horns of the bull

And charge

Rejoicing you will see my smile

Deserving

A life that is not a half-life

Finding

A love that is not a half-love

Take the horns of the bull

And charge

Pandemic

Waves of urgency

In the air

Impending doom

Looming and waiting

Like a storm ready to break

Necks in a row

Long and lean

Fragile and frozen

Like a wine glass

Empty

But the last drops of fermentation

Coats the bottom

Luck has run out

And there's nothing left

But sticky bitterness

Bob Dylan

An old song

Can tickle your bones

And whisper from the inside

I am home

It can bubble up

From deep within

Memorized like the lines

Of a lover's face

And dance from your lips

Like a taste

You never knew you missed

Mutiny

Sailing over waters

Crystal clear and strong

Sailing over hardships

Mistakes and disappointments

Ever-long

Leaving my Co-Captain

On the shore

And in the sand

With nothing to make

And nothing to take

In his weathered hands

"Two is better together" I hear

As the waves rise and fall in crescendo

And fill up my ear

Keeping a weathered eye on the horizon

I don't look back

"This is what you get…

When you don't pick up the slack"

The Times of Change

We hear the wheels

Screeching and slowing down

The rhythm of progress

All across the town

Mothers see their homes

Filling up the empty

Spaces that were

Fathers see their children

For the first time

For whom they are

These are the times of change

We didn't heed the whispers

Of the many warnings

These are the times of change

To count blessings

And number our priorities

When the sun rises in the morning

The Giving Tree

I am a tree

Strong and proud

Offering shade

And a loyal place for life

Offering food

And shelter from the night

I am a tree

Rigid and unyielding

Branches for arms

With nothing to wrap around

Beautifully rooted

Regal queen with a green crown

I am a tree

Rhythmic and generous

Take from me

What you need in the Spring

For in the Winter

When I am cold and alone

The howling wind will be my king

Dressing to Impress

In a dark room

Under the light of the moon

Beautiful and beckoning

You wait

Hanging there with ribbons and bows

Sequins a mirror

Of the twinkle in my eye

Should I try…

Draping the fabric over my skin

So smooth like milk it falls

And I begin

To become the woman you believe

I am

This sham

Hiding in the folds of my dress

Striving in my wish to impress

Upon you

We are made for each other

Play

Curves

Smooth

Squeezing

Teasing

Pushing

Pulling

Slippery

Wet

Hot

And

Lost

In

Ecstasy

Sandpiper's Song

Chasing our moment

Of sand and sun

Frolicking in frivolity and fun

I open my can with a crack

And you grab your snack

From a potato chip sack

Looking out over the waves

We sigh and say

What a perfect beach day

It turned out to be today

Sandpipers come close

And chirp with their song

As we try to escape

From the world what is wrong

The Morning

Dew twinkling

Scrub jay

Singing

Sun

Peeking

Over the trees

                      Breathe in

                      Promise

                      Breathe out

                      Life

                      Nightmares receding

                      From the night

                                          Coffee

                                        Steaming

                                        Head

                                        Dreaming

                                        Of a way

                                        To squeeze out the good

                                        Of this new day

Baiting

The afternoon
When you led me to bed
And opened my legs
And my eyes
To desire

Dining on my lips
Caressing my hips
Wanting nothing in return
But to make me burn

And when you left
The chase began
Consuming me
Like all along
That was your plan

Battlefield

Once a house

Now a war zone

Bracing for battle

And the civilians have all gone

Conversations misfire

Targets avoided

No ammunition left

And the mission is aborted

The pacifist is replaced

By a MIA Killing Machine

The choices one faces

Knee-deep in casualties

The changes one makes

In a 16-year war regime

Ghosts

A house with 4 walls

And 2 wandering people

Wondering what lay in the cards

Dusty and on the mantle

Conversing with shadows

Refusing to touch skin

Hearing only the echoes

Of their own heart

Dust growing thick

Inches by years

The cards are forgotten

All for the sake of fear

Like ghosts they glide

By walls turned hollow

Forgetting what they lived for

Trading their hopes for sorrow

Wishlist

Gentle

Soft spoken

Slow to anger

Strong

Unwavering

Character

Deep

Understanding

Intellectual

Appreciates

Art and

The natural

Innovative

Force

Of energy

Shoulders

Wide enough

To support

Me

The Woodlands

Castles made from trees

For you and me

You'll be the king

And I'll be the queen

And a canopy of leaves is our throne

Dressed in vines and moss

Our breasts across with shine and gloss

And two crowns of forest

As the birds sing their chorus

In fauna tones

Ruling forest and fairies

Dining on berries

Safe in our sanctuary

Where time is nearly stopped and carries

The promise of atonement

The Bloom

Ripe and ready

Radiant and in the sun

Pistil quivers in the wind

And reaches out

A loaded gun

Son of Man

The flash of your teeth

The light in your eyes

I haven't seen them in awhile

Don't retreat!!

Stay for a bit

So I can figure out

Before they split

How to keep them here

Something unzipped the layers

You wear over yourself

And a piece of your soul shone through

What can I do

To keep it here in the sun

And not let it run

Back down into the layers

Of unspoken things unsung

Life's Work

Creating moments like pieces of cloth

Added to a quilt

We sew to our heart's content

Making thoughtful choices to shape our child

In shapes we never became

Like choosing the perfect pattern in creating a masterpiece

Sew sew sewing

See see seeing

Stopping to see the progress in the things they do

Reaping in of what we sow

And swell with pride burying our head back down

Into the work of the quilt

Sew sew sewing

See see seeing

The quilt is done and our child is grown

Into the masterpiece we created

Years of work and careful choosing

But the thread is breaking and the patterns are fading

The quilt is fraying

Our child is alone in the world

Like a sailor without a compass

The weight of our careful choosing didn't outweigh

The absence of the choices unmade

Recipe

She was made

From equal parts

Hard as stone

Unwavering in the storm

And soft as a feather

Ready to break

In my hands

Pearls

My words

Like freshwater pearls

Are not cheap

And do not come freely

Chipping away at the oyster shell

Trading grit

Trading sweat

For a syllable or two

And if you are lucky enough

To come by a string of them

Sparkling and milky smooth

With flecks of iridescent blue

Covet them

They are worth every bit a treasure

Lie freshwater pearls

From the ocean's own bed

Dirty Laundry

Like a crumbled dress

I shed you all at once

And the dreams I had

Like remnants of perfume

Clinging to the fabric

Release

And fade into the air

Courage

Taking courage by the reins

I lay him down

And mount him

Like a stallion

Riding hard and fast

To cover miles

Of loneliness

In my past

The Morning of the Miracle

The breeze carries

A promise of forgiveness

The blooms strain

To show their best face

The deer rest

In peace next to boar

And the child sleeps

Dreaming of baskets

And candy and eggs

Unaware of the cost

Of sacrifice

The Decision

Frozen in time

Like a clock

That no longer chimes

In the same old dance

In the same old circumstance

Fear can bind down

Or fear can set a-flight

And with all her might

Turning her face to the unknown

Shedding all the comfort

Of what feels like home…

She grows wings

And flies

The Storm

The rain falls

Hard and steady

But like the Elephant Ear

That withstands the sting…

Drops bouncing

And rolling between the creases

Of the wide and wavy leaf

Think of it as a shower

And withstand the storm

The Traveler

Like a beacon

Shining over the sea

A drink of rubies

Shines for her

Signaling rest

For the weary traveler

Taking a sip

And gathering strength

For the next leg

Of her journey

Pandemic

Shifty stares

Harsh glares

Buyers beware

Dangerous people

Without a care

Are out there

Everywhere

Femininity

3 Points of power

Sex

Love

And life

A triple decker triad

And our right

As a woman

Carrying

The shape of the goddess

Between our legs

Bestowing blessings

To all of mankind

Miracle

She calls herself

The last rose of summer

Tired, thirsty, and worn

But I call her strength, perseverance,

And a miracle

Like a fruit tree in the desert

And she is me

Ritual

It is Beltane

And the evening wanes

As the goddess awaits

To be taken by the boar

Like years before

And every time

My May bride is chosen

Fresh as a maid

As he lays her down

In a bed of flowers

The hours tick away

And the people play

Rejoicing in the miracle of sacrifice

And then rebirth

Sanctuary

Of pageantry

And planks

Stretching out

My line of sight

Each step an echo

Marking the time

Into the cathedral

Built of leaves and life

Stained glass windows

Of palm fronds

Pews of mangroves

And an alter

Of wild honeysuckle

A place of worship

To the goddess

And the sweet goodness

Of nature

Southern Soul

Billowing with blues

And soul of the soil

From the Mississippi Delta

She is made

From the generations

Of hot and dusty afternoons

After a long day

Out in the fields

She can make beauty

From poverty

And a feast

From famine

A magnificent magnolia

To behold

She is strength

Bending like reeds

Woven together

By the trials of her ancestors

And she will not break

Lost

Like a coin tossed

And forgotten

In the street

And when we meet

You'll be seen

From the bottom

of your shoe

Will you take the time

To pick up and shine

Me down

Restoring my worth

And my truth

Or will you pick me up

And rub me

Between your thumbs

Whispering

A wish of luck

For you

The Traveler

Like a beacon

Shining on the edge of the sea

The juice of rubies

Shines for her

Signaling rest

For the weary traveler

Taking a sip

And gathering strength

For the next leg

Of her journey

What a mighty thing

To travel thousands of miles

Her heart no bigger

Than a piece of shell

Scattered on the shore

Fixer- Upper

Rolling along

For an afternoon drive

Hunting for houses

At half past 5

Walking through

Doors that double

And looking to the sides

I can see our life here

And the happiest of times

You see the holes

You see the work

And days full of strife

You see the hardship

And the smell

No place for your wife

A meeting of the minds

Who will cross the divide

And see the other side

Through the other's eyes

Mother's Day

It is not the gift

Lack of gifts

Or gifts given without a care

It's that in our days

Of probationary stay

To decide what our future will portray

You slept

While your son was waiting on the steps

For the pomp and circumstance

And when there was none

You taught him

This is how you treat your mother

So in the future days of his life

He will remember

This is how I treat my wife

The Reader

Oh the many places

Laid out within the lines

And in between the pages

Wonderful worlds on both sides

They spring from the page

And lift my heart to flight

Transcending space

Thousands of miles in one night

Over golden dunes in Sahara

Over lilac hills in France

Or Rainbow row houses in Havana

No difference is the distance

Crawling between the covers

Knuckles curled around the sides

Devouring every word

Losing myself in the ride

The Fork

Part 1

Walking brisk and with decision

Steering my course for the best position

Staying head fast and moving along

Step by step, sure and strong

When what appears before me, but a fork

Splits the road in two- one west, one north

Oh the agony of indecision

Oh the luxury of having a fixed position

Part 2

Looking closely at the lines as if to see

A message of an answer left for me

One road looks to be more of the same

The road I've traveled, no place for blame

The other road, it looks to bend and wind

Looking a bit hidden, not sure what I'll find

So laid before me two different paths

And my decision to make, no one to ask

I scratch my head and with a deep breath

Pick up my feet and set my tread

The road fully predictable or the road less traveled

Would you choose comfort?

Or would you choose a challenge?

Sheep

In a turquoise wing back chair

Queening and daring

The world with a stare

Like aiming a scope

She looks down her nose

And she knows

Sheep will keep quiet and follow

Like little lambs to their Mary

Neglecting their sorrows

When one hand rules as an iron fist

And the other hand provides

Domesticated bliss

The sheep will turn

Their cheeks and spurn

The rumors of revolt

For their souls they've spoilt

Single Soul

Secret friends

The stars and I

Holding my dreams

Through the night

And when it seems

There isn't a soul

Who knows

The depth of me

I look to them

And their light whispers

To me a hymn

Don't put away the fight

Of your campaign

We are your champion

Until the end of days

Stardust is what you are made

Capitalism

Carried by the waves of society

A hostage to progress am I

On the ebb and flow of industry

Economic distress riptide

Self

Always lurking in the shadows

And nipping at my heels

But sometimes

Out of nowhere

He rises and engulfs me

In his black bell sleeves

And all at once the emptiness

And choices not taken

Left along the road

Cry out to me

Anchoring me to ache

Begging me to fill the void

The Clearing

And so they call to me

The secrets of fairies

Under the rocks

On the edge of the wood

And as the sun shines down

Through canopies of leaves

Awaiting like golden lace

I go deeper still

And lose myself forever

Gone without a trace

www.ingramcontent.com/pod-product-compliance
Lightning Source LLC
LaVergne TN
LVHW031613060526
838201LV00065B/4827